Financially Savvy Girl Inc

Copyright ©2024 by Financially Savvy Girl Inc.
The texts, drawings, and designs are protected by copyright ©2023-2024 Financially Savvy Girl Inc.

Published in 2024 by Financially Savvy Girl Inc. All rights reserved. No part of this book may be copied or used without permission.

Published by Financially Savvy Girl Inc - FSG Publishings
Author: Aquilas K Dapaah
Illustrator: Kusengama Kanyanta
Cover page designed by: Gaetan Joachim
All rights reserved.

About Financially Savvy Girl Inc.

Financially Savvy Girl Inc. is a financial literacy platform founded by the author of this book, Aquilas K Dapaah. This remarkable platform focuses on empowering women by providing them with the confidence and knowledge needed to transform their lives through wisdom, financial intelligence and building a generation capable of passing these skills on to the next.

This book is dedicated to our precious children,
dear godchildren, cousins, nieces and nephews.
May you always take care of what God has
entrusted to you with love and wisdom.

Maman/Tata/Yaya loves you and believes in you.

Once upon a time,
in a loving little home,
lived Uche, a curious 3-year-old boy,
with his family.

One afternoon,
while playing with his toys in his room shared with his big sister, Uche noticed three piggy banks on his sister's shelf.
There was a small one for spending on toys,
a medium one for savings,
and a large piggy bank for investing.

He looked up at his Mama and asked, "Maman, what are these piggy banks for?"

With a warm smile, Mama sat down beside him and explained, "Oh, Uche, these piggy banks help us manage our money. The small one is for spending on toys and treats, the medium one is for saving for something special, and the big one is for investing in our future."

Listening intently, Uche asked, "Can I have my own set of piggy banks like these?

His Mama and Papa exchanged a smile and replied, "Of course, Uche! It's a fantastic way to learn about money. We'll get you your own set, decorate them together, and you can start saving and learning about managing money."

Excitedly, Uche clapped his hands, saying,
"Yay, I am getting my own piggy banks!"

His parents chuckled, "That's wonderful, Uche! You'll have your own piggy banks for spending, saving, and investing. You'll learn how to make smart choices with your money." Papa said.

He chose his 3 piggy banks, painted them and decorated them with his favourite colours! As time passed, Uche learned valuable lessons about money by putting a bit of money in his spending piggy bank, a bit more money in his savings piggy bank and a lot more in his investing piggy bank.

Every few months, something exciting happened. Uche eagerly joined his sister as they gathered their piggy banks and, with their parents' guidance, he began a journey to shape his future.

First, he opened the smallest piggy bank for toys. Uche counted the coins inside and realised he had enough to buy a new toy. He felt proud because he set a goal and achieved it.

Next was the medium-sized savings piggy bank. Uche collected his saved $20 bills. Instead of spending, he added this money in a high interest savings account that his parents had set up for him for emergencies. It was all about being prepared for unexpected needs.

Finally, it was time for the large investment piggy bank. Uche watched the money grow and, with his parents' help, he used it to buy shares of a company he admired, learning about patience and smart choices in investing.

With each cycle of spending, saving, and investing, Uche gained a deeper understanding of money. He knew these lessons would help him create a bright and responsible future, where he could achieve his dreams wisely.

Through his piggy bank adventures, Uche grew up knowing how to not spend all his money, he learned to save for tomorrow and invest for the future.

As he keeps growing and discovering more and more about the importance of saving and investing, Uche cannot wait to tell us all about compound interest in his next adventure.

Uche's story with his piggy banks teaches us the importance of learning about money and making responsible choices. It shows us that by being smart with money, we can build a secure and successful future.

The End.

Copyright @2024 Financially Savvy Girl Inc.

About the Author

Meet Aquilas K Dapaah, the author, lawyer, mom, wife and wealth mentor who is dedicated to empowering people to build generational wealth. She is the CEO & Founder of Financially Savvy Girl Inc and co-founder of The Women Investors Network Canada.

Years ago, Aquilas found herself in a challenging situation, burdened by a six-figure debt after law school and lacking the knowledge and skills to navigate the world of finance. However, she refused to let her circumstances define her future. With an unwavering commitment to change her financial trajectory, she embarked on a transformative path.

Through dedicated learning and relentless effort, Aquilas acquired the financial literacy and expertise needed to turn her life around and paid off the six figure debt in 2.5 years and she went on to build a multi 7 figure net-worth business in just a few years.
She harnessed her experiences, both the triumphs and the setbacks, as valuable lessons that shaped her mindset and propelled her forward. Driven by her compassionate heart, Aquilas expanded her horizons to become a mindset & wealth mentor, recognizing the importance of cultivating a strong and positive mental attitude in achieving financial success. She believes that every child has the potential to be a powerful agent of change, capable of building a brighter future.

In her delightful financially savvy girl Inc children's book series, Aquilas takes young readers, parents, guardians and educators on an enchanting journey, through relatable characters and captivating stories, she imparts essential lessons on financial literacy, the power of positive thinking, and the value of helping others.
Aquilas' unique blend of legal expertise, coaching skills, and a heart full of empathy allows her to connect with children and adults alike, inspiring them to believe in their abilities and pursue their dreams fearlessly. She fosters a nurturing environment where children feel empowered to take control of their financial destinies, ensuring a brighter future for themselves and generations to come.
Whether she is in the courtroom, coaching clients, or penning inspiring stories, Aquilas stands as a beacon of hope, reminding us all that with the right mindset, knowledge, discipline and determination, we can change our money story, build generational wealth and live our wealthier lives with wisdom and intelligence.

Other books by this author:

www.ingramcontent.com/pod-product-compliance
Lightning Source LLC
Chambersburg PA
CBHW041707160426
43209CB00017B/1769